ALCHEMY
CONTEMPORARY
JEWELLERY
FROM
BRITAIN

SOLANGE
AZAGURY—PARTRIDGE
NAOMI FILMER
TANVI KANT
ANDREW LAMB
SHAUN LEANE
LINA PETERSON
LAURA POTTER
SCOTT WILSON

FOREWORD

As the British Council's Art, Architecture & Design team thought hard about how to extend our ten-year old design programme into the Middle East, it was no co-incidence that jewellery came to everyone's mind. Although undoubtedly influenced by the stereotypical bejewelled riches of the East, we had more strategically acute reasons. In this region gold is an unequivocally vivid and significant commodity; jewellery is an important and universally-acknowledged social signifier; and fine craft traditions of jewellery-making go back centuries. How fascinating to compare these firm traditions of value with our own more distorted and pluralistic consumer culture. A culture in which inherited notions of value and beauty have been so creatively challenged by a range of movements from Pop Art to Punk Rock and Postmodernism.

This British aesthetic history is what we have attempted to capture in the title *Alchemy*, which (in both English and Arabic) refers to the renaissance practice – part science, part black magic – by which it was believed that low-grade metals could be transmuted into gold. The exhibition curators, Dana Andrew and Alison Moloney, allude more fully to this concept as they describe the eight young jewellers' work in the following pages. We are grateful to Judith Clark and Charlie Smith for giving form to *Alchemy's* underlying themes with their exceptionally sensitive design of the exhibition and catalogue.

It is the British Council's purpose to build mutually beneficial relationships between the United Kingdom and other countries. The fast-developing cultural infrastructure of the Middle East, and the Gulf States in particular, breeds exciting opportunities for knowledge-sharing and exchange between the region's creative practitioners and their counterparts in the UK. Such opportunities are particularly fertile in the context of a growing recognition of the creative industries: those sectors (design for example) that exploit knowledge, entrepreneurship and adaptive, creative-thinking. For this reason the exhibition contains a commercial as well as a cultural message. As well as celebrating sheer creativity in art, craft and design, *Alchemy* aims to make a strong case for jewellery as one of the creative industries with significant potential for commercial growth in the Middle East. A diverse programme of workshops, lectures and events is being developed for each country, with an emphasis on education and the business aspects of design. This programme is being developed in close consultation with our arts managers in the six countries to which *Alchemy* will tour. We especially acknowledge the support of Jamal al Moosawi-Hassanovich in making this exhibition of contemporary jewellery from the UK a reality in the Middle East.

EMILY CAMPBELL HEAD OF
DESIGN & ARCHITECTURE
BRITISH COUNCIL ARTS GROUP

ALCHEMY: CONTEMPORARY JEWELLERY FROM BRITAIN

Alchemy presents a range of jewellers, from recent graduates to names well-established in the industries of jewellery and fashion. This selection is not intended as an overview of British jewellery, but instead it offers eight individual perspectives of contemporary jewellery practice. Solange Azagury-Partridge, Naomi Filmer, Tanvi Kant, Andrew Lamb, Shaun Leane, Lina Peterson, Laura Potter and Scott Wilson all challenge conventional parameters of jewellery design by experimenting with materials, references and scale, and by questioning our inherited notions of value, identity and adornment.

Britain made a name for itself in the world of contemporary jewellery in the 70s and 80s with the work of jewellers such as Wendy Ramshaw, David Watkins, Susanna Heron and Caroline Broadhead. This generation of designers expanded the concept of jewellery through the materials and techniques they used and the questionable wearability of the forms they created. Their departure from tradition had a lasting effect, and a new generation of designers and makers continues to broaden the scope and question the meaning of jewellery in Britain in varied and surprising ways.

Azagury-Partridge has brought her design aesthetic to major brands on the high street as well as leading luxury jewellers. Her one-off collection for H&M made exclusive designs available to the mass market while her work for Boucheron opened up this traditional brand to a more fashion-conscious consumer. These collaborations highlight the prestige of the Azagury-Partridge brand name.

Filmer seeks to evoke emotion through her work, often affecting the posture of the wearer through her designs or the materials from which the jewellery is made. She often casts the negative spaces of the body – the "in-between" parts - to create prosthetic-like pieces, or uses materials that react with the body rather than simply adorning it. Her Chocolate and Ice collections dissolve at body temperature creating tactile but ephemeral pieces. As the forms dissolve the physical effects of the materials remain on the skin.

Kant's jewellery, made from reclaimed textiles, is led by the process of making rather than directly interpreting drawings and studies. Although the same technical methods might be employed to make each piece, the inherent quality of the materials dictates the form and character of her work. In addition to fine sari fabrics, Kant works with cotton and synthetic textiles which bring a more physical quality to her work. Her neckpieces can be worn on the body in a variety of ways, the continuous, springing loops energetically winding their way around the neck, torso or arm.

Lamb is the only jeweller in the exhibition working solely in precious metals. He is able to create jewellery with shimmering optical effects by combining different textures and colours. When formed and soldered together, the physical properties of wire add to these effects by creating their own patterns of light and shade. The viewer becomes engaged in a game of hide and seek; from one side, a ring could appear to be made completely of silver or platinum while from the other side, completely made of gold. Every move of the body allows a different perspective of the piece.

During his seven-year apprenticeship in London's jewellery quarter, Hatton Garden, Leane learned the painstaking craft of goldsmithing, creating work for companies such as Asprey and private clients including the Sultan of Brunei. After being introduced to fashion designer Alexander McQueen, Leane was spurred on to teach himself silversmithing in order to produce outlandish pieces for the catwalk – much to the amusement of his former craftsmen masters. As the spectacle of McQueen's presentations grew so did the stature of Leane's own work

Peterson combines the traditional handmade techniques of stitching, embroidery and crochet with the industrial process of dip coating. This industrial application is used to striking effect, producing bright and tactile pieces that conceal a precious interior of metals and Swarovski crystals known only to the wearer and maker. Peterson originally created the dipped metal structures to act as an anchor for the collaged and stitched materials but quickly realised the beauty of these intriguingly-shaped structures as objects in their own right.

Potter's new collection of work continues to explore accepted ideas of value. *Lifetime Medals* is a series constructed from second-hand gold that Potter has purchased on eBay. Each medal is comprised of one single 'lot' of items that may or may not have belonged to one person, raising questions about sentimental value and ownership. Purchasing jewellery anonymously on eBay subverts our ideas about jewellery as an intimate commodity and we are left to construct a mental image of an 'owner' connecting the pieces.

Wilson was commissioned to make his first catwalk pieces as a millinery student on a work placement with the fashion designer Karl Lagerfeld. The fashion studio had no conventional millinery equipment or materials and so Wilson produced unstructured headpieces from materials sourced from the local department store. Piano wire and wire mesh were combined to create the distressed and spiky headwear. While working on his commercial collections, Wilson is still enticed by the fashion designers and the stylists who commission him to produce work that will enhance and complete the fashion story of the season.

DANA ANDREW AND
ALISON MOLONEY

ADORNMENT IN THE
21ST CENTURY

The variety and exuberance of our contemporary jewellery demonstrates
a heritage that runs deep in the culture and history of Britain. The mutable
culture of adornment over the past century and the commitment of
educational institutions to developing the original creative voices of
generation after generation have both ensured the potential of jewellery
as an important medium for creative expression. Today, there are many
schools of thought about what jewellery might be; and the possibilities
for material practice are unbounded.

It was during the 50s that modernist ideas within European art, architecture
and design became absorbed into the industrial mainstream, better understood
and more popular. After the Second World War, events like the Festival of
Britain in 1951 were deliberate attempts by the state to inspire a generation to
build a future that integrated new design ideas. Science and technology, and a
decorative and modernist aesthetic, were promoted as utopian lifestyle choices.

The post-war return to consumption in the late 50s and early 60s saw
young designers opening fashion boutiques which made their accessible

BELOW
VIEW OF THE DOME OF
DISCOVERY BUILT FOR
THE FESTIVAL OF BRITAIN
OPENED 4 MAY 1951

to a wider audience. Jewellery was invited to join this retail revolution: experimental boutiques such as Mary Quant's Bazaar stocked an eclectic mix of clothes, accessories and jewellery and department stores supported new ideas.

This was also the legendary era of Britain's art-schools, during which jewellery design education developed from a traditional to an experimental approach. Vocational trade education for jewellers going back 800 years had traditionally offered pupils a seven year apprenticeship. Pupils would learn the technical skills of an historical craft from a workshop master who might specialise in stone setting, wax carving or enamelling. Today, few apprenticeships of this kind are taken up; most students elect instead to learn jewellery design at art schools.

Gerda Flockinger, originally a printmaker, became Britain's iconic figure in experimental jewellery in the 50s. As head of a new jewellery course at Hornsey College of Art in 1961, during its period as Britain's most revolutionary and archetypical 60s art school, Flockinger's course was defiantly different to the trade education. She borrowed models of thinking and exploration from the fine arts and combined these with fine jewellery-making skills; an approach that influenced a generation of jewellers and teaching professionals across Britain. The effect of her teaching can also be traced in the increasingly inter-disciplinary fields of fashion and fine art, for example in the innovative work of sculptor-jeweller-performance artist and Hornsey student Julia Mannheim. Art colleges today continue to teach jewellery-making skills alongside design, drawing, and cultural and historical criticism.

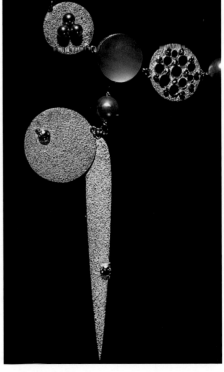

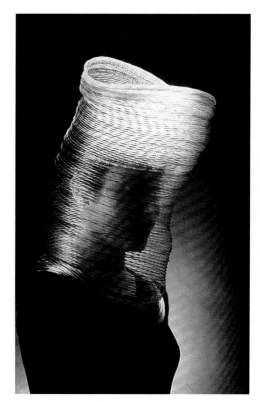
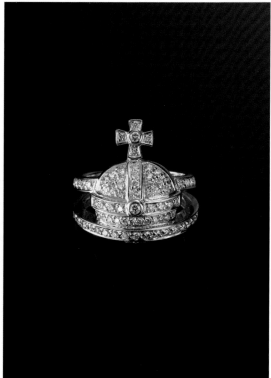

New critical approaches to visual culture emerged in the 60s and 70s, including a questioning of what bodily adornment might mean for both artist and wearer. This period saw a jewellery revolution in Germany and the Netherlands. The futuristic, over-scaled, polished aluminium pieces of Dutch designers Gijs Bakker and Emmy van Leersum, among others, had begun to challenge historical value systems and to inspire cross-European conversations and collaborations. As these experimental jewellers' networks expanded to include the United States and Japan, the discipline began to mature and produce work that reflected a global context. A commercial platform for such work was eventually realised in the 1970s when galleries such as Electrum, in London's South Molton Street, and Galerie Ra, in Amsterdam, were established. The founders of these galleries gave jewellers like Bakker and van Leersum wide creative freedom and a significant platform to influence others.

Meanwhile in the UK Caroline Broadhead, Susanna Heron and Pierre Degan responded to the anti-authoritarian political and cultural climate of the late 70s by rejecting traditional materials. Embracing the non-precious – paper, nylon, perspex and rubber – they radically challenged accepted ideas of what jewellery might be. Out of this challenge arose the idea of the body as an arena or a canvas; for example Susanna Heron's work, inspired by her viewing of Oscar Schlemmer's Bauhuas performances at the Central School of Art & Design in the 60s, refined pieces by using the body as a surface in itself.

At the same time as this artist-jeweller was becoming a reality, the influence of industrial design – new processes like anodising aluminium, neoprene

ABOVE LEFT
CAROLINE BROADHEAD
VEIL NECKPIECE 1983
NYLON MONOFILAMENT
ABOVE RIGHT
VIVIENNE WESTWOOD
ORB RING 2005
WHITE GOLD AND DIAMONDS

rubber-coating and titanium surface colouring – allowed a fledgling commercial production industry to expand. Unwilling to embrace new approaches to jewellery design and manufacture, many 19th century mass production facilities in the industrial towns of Birmingham, Sheffield, Glasgow and Edinburgh ceased trading. In the wake of their demise, newly-graduated jewellers became significant in British jewellery manufacture. Small ateliers, driven by design and innovation, became increasingly common and were ideally placed to service the new British fashion designers of the 80s as the stock markets boomed. Jeweller Reema Pachachi's work with major New York fashion designers enjoyed major exposure, while in London, Stephen King of S-Tek Design worked with Richmond-Cornejo and Louise Sant accessorised numerous collections for English Eccentrics.

Alongside the compulsively experimental cultures of art and craft in Britain, this relationship between jewellery and fashion remains a significant force behind creative and commercial innovation today. Throughout history, jewellery has been as acute an index of fashion as clothing. Jeweller, Peter Page collaborated with fashion designer Ossie Clark in the 70s to create spectacular gold face masks and Mick Milligan accessorised Zandra Rhodes' collections with bold baroque jewels. Such collaborations have become conventional for the fashion and jewellery industries. A jeweller can heighten and accent the "story" of the collection, while in turn the profile of a fashion designer brings the jeweller's work to the attention of the big international audience that fashion enjoys. Clothing and jewellery have become mutually dependent: Simon Harrison's production work for Vivienne Westwood has contributed to the commercial success of the brand; and Shaun Leane's collaborative work with Alexander McQueen captures headlines.

Meanwhile jewellery and accessories play an increasingly important commercial role for luxury brands. Just as traditional fashion brands like Burberry and John Smedley have reinvigorated their collections by employing young talent, so have traditional luxury jewellery houses. Reema Pachachi created the influential aesthetic vision for the new diamond house of De Beers LV, while Solange Azagury-Partridge brought a fashionable edge to high-end jewellery brand Boucheron. Such collaborations have enriched the vision of these businesses while appealing to a younger and more fashion-conscious consumer.

Today, lively critical discourse in Britain enables jewellers to explore the best expression of an idea with extraordinary freedom; and to interrogate inherited notions of value, wearability and beauty in outstandingly liberated ways. At the same time the visual language of contemporary jewellery is continually enriched by the imported skills and knowledge of an increasing number of European and Asian students attracted by the freedom of British design schools. The wider context is an ever-changing array of exhibitions, lectures, conferences and retail initiatives that inspires and encourages jewellers to be bold in their visions for how one might be adorned in the early years of the 21st century.

SIMON FRASER
LONDON, SEPTEMBER 2006

BELOW
LAPÉROUSE RING
BEAUTÉ DANGEREUSE
COLLECTION 2002
DIAMONDS AND PLATINUM
SOLANGE AZAGURY-PARTRIDGE
FOR BOUCHERON
RIGHT
STAR SPINNER RING 1998
18CT WHITE GOLD AND
DIAMONDS

ABOVE LEFT
HEART OF GOLD PENDANT 2005
18CT YELLOW GOLD
ABOVE RIGHT
BLUE BIRD RING 2005
18CT YELLOW GOLD AND ENAMEL

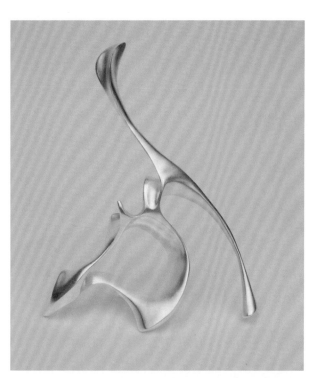

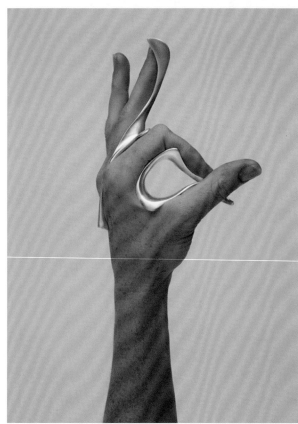

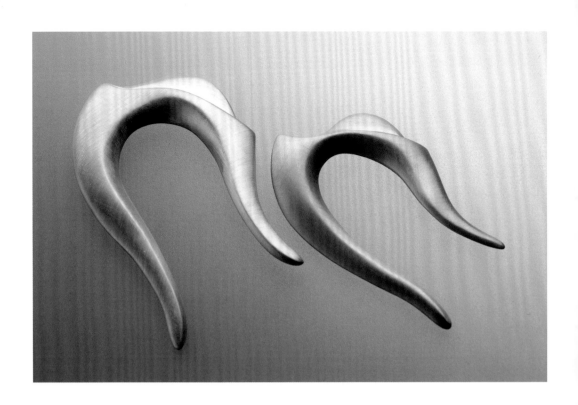

LEFT AND ABOVE LEFT
HAND MANIPULATION PIECE 1993
CAST SILVER

ABOVE
TULIP FINGER—BETWEEN 1995
CAST SILVER

ABOVE
MULTICOLOURED NECKPIECE
2006
SARI FABRIC, YARN AND
PORCELAIN
RIGHT
NECKPIECE (LONG BLUE
WITH HOOPS) 2006
SARI FABRIC, YARN AND
PORCELAIN

TANVI KANT

Tanvi Kant makes jewellery using reclaimed textiles, such as pieces from her mother's old saris, unwanted furnishing fabrics or her own clothes, which she combines with hand-formed pieces of single-fired porcelain. Kant's choice of materials refers to recycling and sustainability but they also give reference to more personal and collective histories.

The contemplative nature of the pieces derives from the simple and repetitive techniques employed by Kant to bind, knot, whip and sew multiple units together. Although transformed, the fabrics can be glimpsed in their original form through the fastenings of the pieces. Kant often leaves the ends of her neck pieces in a raw state, allowing the wearer to feel and remember the origins of the work. Kant's work has evolved from diverse sources and influences: the physical structure of her pieces being influenced by the study of plant cell structures as much as the study of ethnographic tools, and the association of adornment with cultural and religious rituals.

Yellow Wrap Neckpiece, produced for Kant's degree show is one of the first pieces Kant made using sari fabric. The transformation of the sari, which belonged to Kant's mother, is a poignant stage in its life-cycle, echoing the way that pieces of jewellery with personal or monetary value are often passed down generations of the same family.

WWW.TANVIKANT.CO.UK
BORN 1982 IN BOLTON, UK
LIVES AND WORKS IN LEICESTER, UK

EDUCATION
2005 BA (HONS) 3D DESIGN (SUSTAINABLE
PRACTICE), UNIVERSITY OF DERBY
2003 DIP. OF H.E. DECORATIVE ARTS,
NOTTINGHAM TRENT UNIVERSITY

SELECTED EXHIBITIONS
2007 SOLO EXHIBITION, THE CITY GALLERY,
LEICESTER
2006 GROUP JEWELLERY EXHIBITION, RICHARD
DENNIS GALLERY, LONDON

MIDSUMMER MADNESS: 35TH ANNIVERSARY
SHOW, ELECTRUM GALLERY, LONDON
CRAFTSMANSHIP AND DESIGN AWARDS,
GOLDSMITHS' HALL, LONDON
2005 RUFFORD CRAFT CENTRE, NOTTINGHAMSHIRE
DECONSTRUCT: RECONSTRUCT, BILSTON CRAFT
GALLERY, WEST MIDLANDS
CRACKER, KATH LIBBERT JEWELLERY, SHIPLEY
CHRISTMAS SHOW, ELECTRUM GALLERY, LONDON

SELECTED AWARDS / PRIZES
2005 PROFESSIONAL DEVELOPMENT GRANT,
ARTS COUNCIL OF ENGLAND
NEW DESIGNERS ASSOCIATION FOR
CONTEMPORARY JEWELLERS' AWARD

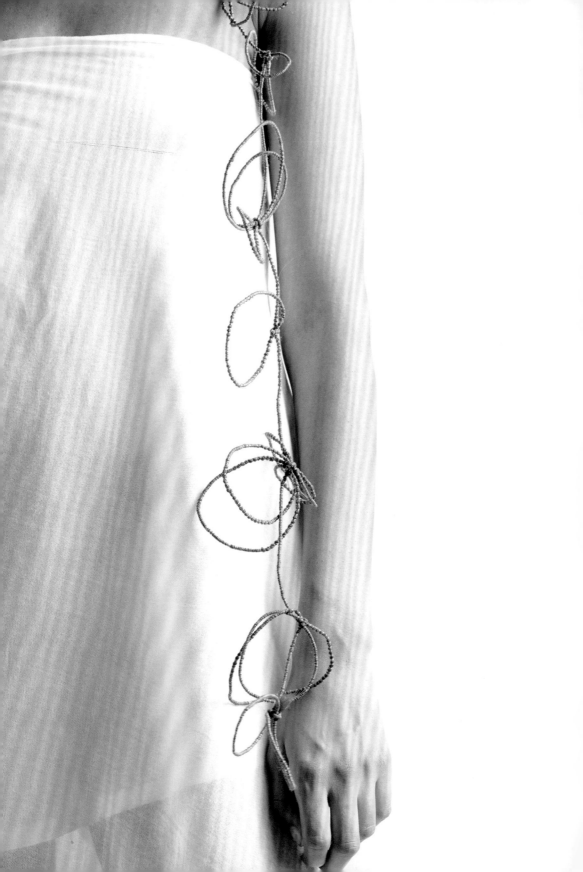

LEFT
GREEN KNOTTED WRAP 2006
(SYNTHETIC) TEXTILE
AND YARN
ABOVE RIGHT
MULTICOLOURED NECKPIECE
2006
SARI FABRIC, YARN AND
PORCELAIN (DETAIL)

BELOW
OPTICAL PENDANT 2001
18CT YELLOW GOLD
RIGHT
AMETHYST EARRINGS 2005
18CT YELLOW GOLD AND
AMETHYST

BELOW
BROOCH 2004
18CT YELLOW AND RED GOLD
RIGHT
OPTICAL NECKLACE 2001
18CT YELLOW GOLD

LEFT
IVORY RESIN BANGLE 2004
SILVER, RED TOPAZ AND
IVORY RESIN
RIGHT
ROSE CORSET
SHAUN LEANE FOR GIVENCHY
SPRING/SUMMER 2000
SILVER

SHAUN LEANE

The scale of Shaun Leane's jewellery varies dramatically from small commercial pieces to full body sculptures. His work – like that of his catwalk collaborator, fashion designer Alexander McQueen – can have dark undertones which are executed with dramatic effect. His work is both hard-edged yet refined, combining organic form with sharp lines. His collection, *Hook My Heart*, exemplifies his design ethos; a ruby-encrusted heart is pierced through the centre by a thorn-shaped hook. The dramatically oversized *Silver Hook Earrings* are a fashion statement only softened by craftsmanship and an elegant curve. A distinct colour palette of red, black and ivory, which runs throughout his collections, adds an androgynous aspect to his work.

It was his work as an apprentice restoring antique Art Deco and Victorian jewellery that ignited his appreciation for design. Leane became fascinated by the way in which jewellery is as much a document of period styles as fashion itself. Leane's collaboration with McQueen grew out of a shared affinity and appreciation for each other's craft. Both had taken traditional routes into design: McQueen as an apprentice in Savile Row, Leane as an apprentice in Hatton Garden. Their prolific collaboration continues to this day.

WWW.SHAUNLEANE.COM
BORN 1969 IN LONDON
LIVES AND WORKS IN LONDON

EDUCATION
1985–98 ENGLISH TRADITIONAL JEWELLERY CO.
– APPRENTICESHIP AND FULL TIME EMPLOYMENT
AS JEWELLERY MAKER FOCUSING ON DIAMOND
MOUNTING AND ANTIQUE RESTORATION.

SELECTED EXHIBITIONS AND COMMISSIONS
2006 ANGLOMANIA, THE METROPOLITAN
MUSEUM OF ART, NEW YORK
LOVE & WAR, FASHION INSTITUTE OF
TECHNOLOGY, NEW YORK
2005 HISTORY OF DIAMONDS EXHIBITION,
NATURAL HISTORY MUSEUM, LONDON
2004 BODY EXTENSIONS, MUSEUM BELLERIVE,
ZÜRICH, SWITZERLAND
2003 PAST AND PRESENT, JEWELLERY BY 20TH
CENTURY ARTISTS – COLLABORATION WITH
SAM TAYLOR WOOD, LOUISA GUINNESS

GALLERY, LONDON
RUNWAY ROCKS, CATWALK SHOW OF COUTURE
ACCESSORIES SPONSORED BY SWAROVSKI
2002 DESIGNING OURSELVES, NATIONAL
MUSEUM OF SCOTLAND, EDINBURGH
2001 RADICAL FASHION – FASHION IN
MOTION, VICTORIA & ALBERT MUSEUM, LONDON
1999 VIOLENTLY ELEGANT, AURUM, LONDON
1998 NO PICNIC, CRAFTS COUNCIL, LONDON
1995–PRESENT ALEXANDER MCQUEEN,
JEWELLERY AND SCULPTURES–CATWALK
COLLECTION

SELECTED AWARDS / PRIZES
2006 LUXURY JEWELLERY OF THE YEAR, UK
JEWELLERY AWARDS
2005 JEWELLERY DESIGNER OF THE YEAR, UK
JEWELLERY AWARDS
2004 JEWELLERY DESIGNER OF THE YEAR, UK
JEWELLERY AWARDS
2002 TAHITIAN PEARL DESIGN AWARD

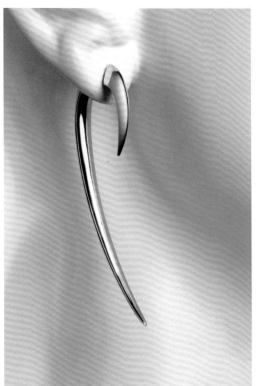

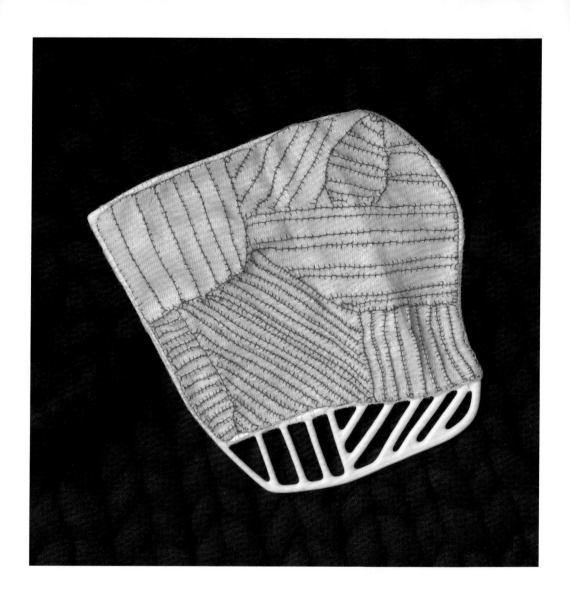

ABOVE
STITCHED BROOCH 2006
DIP COATED METAL AND TEXTILE
ABOVE RIGHT
CROCHETED BROOCH 2006
GOLD PLATED SILVER AND WOOL

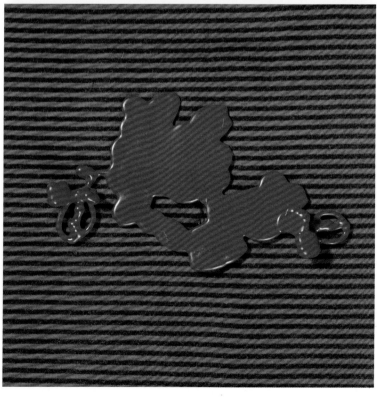

ABOVE LEFT
DIPPED BROOCH 2006
DIP-COATED METAL AND
SWAROVSKI CRYSTALS
LEFT
DIPPED BROOCH 2006
DIP-COATED METAL AND
SWAROVSKI CRYSTALS

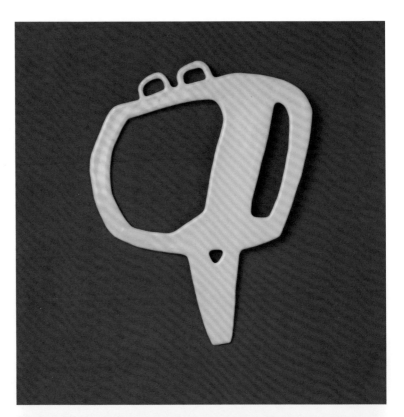

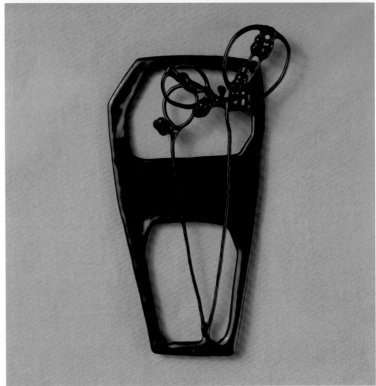

ABOVE RIGHT
DIPPED BROOCH 2006
DIP-COATED METAL
RIGHT
DIPPED BROOCH (3) 2006
DIP-COATED METAL AND
SWAROVSKI CRYSTALS

ABOVE
PRICEY 1998
PAPER AND SILVER
RIGHT
LIFETIME MEDAL
8901815476 2006
9CT GOLD, 18CT GOLD
AND ANTIQUE RIBBON

ABOVE
FISHING WIDOW PARURE 2006
NON-TOXIC FISHING
WEIGHTS, NYLON AND BRASS
SWIVELS

ABOVE LEFT
ALCHEMY 03 2006
9CT GOLD, FINE GOLD
AND LEAD
ABOVE RIGHT
LOCK RING 2004
9CT GOLD AND BRASS PADLOCK

LEFT
DECO NECKLACE
AUTUMN/WINTER 2006
ACRYLIC AND GOLD PLATED
SILVER CHAIN
RIGHT
HEAD PIECE
SCOTT WILSON FOR
HUSSEIN CHALAYAN
SPRING/SUMMER 1999
ACRYLIC

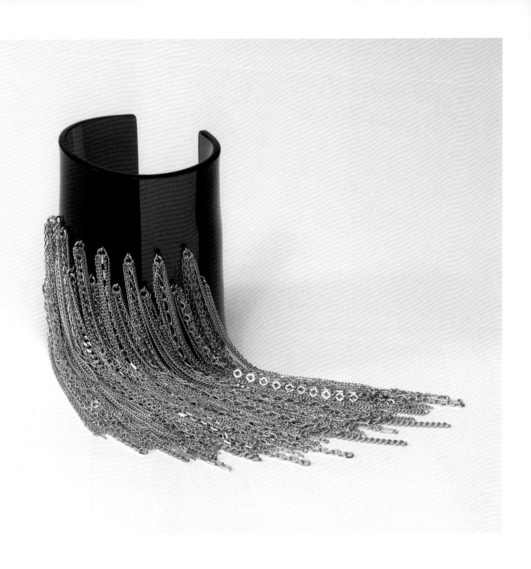

ABOVE
CHAIN FRINGE CUFF
SPRING/SUMMER 1998
ACRYLIC AND SILVER CHAIN
FAR RIGHT
BODY PIECE 2006
ACRYLIC

PICTURE CREDITS

ESSAY
PAGE 1 — © THE BRIDGEMAN ART LIBRARY (PHOTOGRAPHER UNKNOWN)
PAGE 2 — BAZAAR © GETTY IMAGES
SOLANGE AZAGURY–PARTRIDGE
PORTRAIT — LAURENCE ELLIS
PAGE 1 — © BOUCHERON
PAGE 2,3 — LAURENCE ELLIS
PAGE 4 — RODNEY TODD–WHITE AND SONS
NAOMI FILMER
PORTRAIT — WIG TYSMANS
PAGE 1 — GERO CACCIATORE
PAGE 2 — JEREMY FORSTER
PAGE 4 — © CHRIS MOORE
TANVI KANT
PAGE 2,3 — TAS KYPRIANOU
ANDREW LAMB
PAGE 1 — RODNEY TODD–WHITE AND SONS
PAGE 2,3,4 — KEITH LEIGHTON
SHAUN LEANE
PAGE 1,3,4 — TIM BRIGHTMORE
PAGE 2 — © CHRIS MOORE
LINA PETERSON
PORTRAIT — MARCUS ROSS
PAGE 1,2,3,4 — RODNEY TODD–WHITE AND SONS
LAURA POTTER
PAGE 1 — RODNEY TODD–WHITE AND SONS
SCOTT WILSON
PORTRAIT — PHILIP AVIERINOS
PAGE 1,3 — RODNEY TODD–WHITE AND SONS
PAGE 2 — © CHRIS MOORE
PAGE 4 — © RICHARD BUSH, STYLIST SARAH RICHARDSON, FOR i–D MAGAZINE (ISSUE NO.270)

ACKNOWLEDGEMENTS

EXHIBITION ORGANISED BY THE BRITISH COUNCIL'S ART, ARCHITECTURE & DESIGN TEAM.

EXHIBITION CURATORS ALISON MOLONEY AND DANA ANDREW, BRITISH COUNCIL
CURATORIAL ADVISOR SIMON FRASER
EXHIBITION DESIGN JUDITH CLARK
GRAPHIC DESIGN CHARLIE SMITH DESIGN
EXHIBITION FABRICATOR SAM FORSTER LTD
REGIONAL ARTS PROJECT MANAGER, MIDDLE EAST JAMAL AL MOOSAWI-HASSANOVICH
HEAD OF DESIGN & ARCHITECTURE EMILY CAMPBELL, BRITISH COUNCIL
DIRECTOR VISUAL ARTS ANDREA ROSE, BRITISH COUNCIL

CATALOGUE © BRITISH COUNCIL
ILLUSTRATIONS © THE ARTISTS
CATALOGUE ESSAY © SIMON FRASER
INTRODUCTION AND CATALOGUE TEXTS © ALISON MOLONEY, DANA ANDREW

DESIGNED BY CHARLIE SMITH DESIGN
PRINTED BY BAS PRINTERS

PUBLISHED 2006
BRITISH COUNCIL
10 SPRING GARDENS
LONDON SW1A 2BN

WWW.BRITISHCOUNCIL.ORG

ISBN 0 86355 583 7

DISTRIBUTED BY
CORNERHOUSE PUBLICATIONS
70 OXFORD STREET
MANCHESTER M1 5NH

THE ORGANISERS WOULD LIKE TO THANK ALL THE INDIVIDUALS, DESIGNERS AND COMPANIES
WHO HAVE KINDLY LENT ITEMS AND ASSISTED IN THE PREPARATION OF THE EXHIBITION:
SOLANGE AZAGURY-PARTRIDGE, (SOLANGE AZAGURY-PARTRIDGE AND COZETTE MCCREERY),
HUSSEIN CHALAYAN, VALERY DEMURE, NADIA EL-SEBAI, NAOMI FILMER, GIVENCHY, SORREL
HERSHBERG, KARINE HOCKING, CATHERINE INCE, TANVI KANT, ANDREW LAMB, SHAUN LEANE
(SHAUN LEANE AND NANCY WONG), J & C MARTIN, LINA PETERSON, LAURA POTTER, WILL SORRELL,
SWAROVSKI (BEANY GAY), SEAN WILLIAMS, SCOTT WILSON.